CELEBRATING
CHRISTMAS
WITH
JESUS

AN ADVENT DEVOTIONAL

MAX LUCADO

A

Since 1798

Celebrating Christmas with Jesus
© 2011 by Max Lucado

Published in Nashville, Tennessee, by Thomas Nelson®. Thomas Nelson is a trademark of Thomas Nelson, Inc.

Thomas Nelson, Inc., titles may be purchased in bulk for educational, business, fund-raising, or sales promotional use. For information, please e-mail SpecialMarkets@ThomasNelson.com.

Scripture quotations are taken from THE NEW KING JAMES VERSION. © 1982, 1992 by Thomas Nelson, Inc. Used by permission. All rights reserved.

Cover design by ThinkPen Design
Interior design by Kristy L. Morell

ISBN-13: 978-1-4003-1829-2

ISBN-13: 978-1-4003-1828-5 (with display)

Printed in the United States of America

11 12 13 14 15 DP 5 4 3 2 1

www.thomasnelson.com

INTRODUCTION

It was a night like no other. A night that forever punctuated the timeline of history. A night that introduced hope to humanity.

God became man and came into our world—to live as we do and to know laughter and tears, pain and joy, hurt and compassion. His story is a collection of monumental moments that remind us that Christ cared enough to experience life with us. Some moments show us he loves us enough to change the course of hopeless situations—a lunchbucket of fish and bread that fed thousands, a leper's skin made babysoft. Other moments show us he understands our questions and our crying out—the death of a dear friend, the grief of a parent, the garden of agony.

Christmas is the time to remember that Christ not only came, but he stayed, he lived, he cared. Christmas is more than one remarkable event. It was . . . the beginning.

TABLE OF CONTENTS

JESUS' BIRTH

And the Word became flesh and dwelt among us, and we beheld His glory, the glory as of the only begotten of the Father, full of grace and truth.

For the law was given through Moses, but grace and truth came through Jesus Christ. No one has seen God at any time. The only begotten Son, who is in the bosom of the Father, He has declared Him.

JOHN 1:14, 17–18

It all happened in a moment, a most remarkable moment that was like none other. For through that segment of time a spectacular thing occurred. God became a man. While the creatures of earth walked unaware, Divinity arrived. Heaven opened herself and placed her most precious one in a human womb.

God as a fetus. Holiness sleeping in a womb. The creator of life being created. God was given eyebrows, elbows, two kidneys, and a spleen. He stretched against the walls and floated in the amniotic fluids of his mother.

God had come near. No silk. No ivory. No hype. To think of Jesus in such a light is—well, it seems almost irreverent, doesn't it? It is much easier to keep the humanity out of the incarnation.

But don't do it. For heaven's sake, don't. Let him be as human as he intended to be. Let him into the mire and muck of our world. For only if we let him in can he pull us out. †

FROM: *GOD CAME NEAR*

JESUS' BAPTISM AND THE WITNESS OF JOHN

The next day John saw Jesus coming toward him, and said, "Behold! The Lamb of God who takes away the sin of the world! This is He of whom I said, 'After me comes a Man who is preferred before me, for He was before me.' I did not know Him; but that He should be revealed to Israel, therefore I came baptizing with water."

And John bore witness, saying, "I saw the Spirit descending from heaven like a dove, and He remained upon Him. I did not know Him, but He who sent me to baptize with water said to me, 'Upon whom you see the Spirit descending, and remaining on Him, this is He who baptizes with the Holy Spirit.' And I have seen and testified that this is the Son of God."

JOHN 1:29–34

⚬⚬⚬

John the Baptist saw a dove and believed. James Whittaker saw a sea gull and believed. James Whittaker was a member of the hand-picked crew that flew the B-17 Flying Fortress captained by Eddie Rickenbacker. Anybody who remembers October of 1942 remembers the day Rickenbacker and his crew were reported lost at sea.

Somewhere over the Pacific, out of radio range, the plane ran out of fuel and crashed into the ocean. The nine men spent the next months floating in three rafts. They battled the heat, the storms, and the water. Sharks, some ten feet long, would ram their nine-foot boats. After only eight days their rations were eaten or destroyed by saltwater. It would take a miracle to survive.

One morning after their daily devotions, Rickenbacker leaned his head back against the raft and pulled his hat over his eyes. A bird landed on his head. He peered out from under his hat. Every eye was on him. He instinctively knew it was a sea gull.

Rickenbacker caught it, and the crew ate it. The bird's intestines were used for bait to catch fish . . . and the crew survived to tell the story. A story about a stranded crew with no hope or help in sight. A story about prayers offered and prayers answered. A story of salvation. But the greatest event of that day was not the rescue of a crew but the rescue of a soul.

James Whittaker was an unbeliever. The plane crash didn't change his unbelief. The days facing death didn't cause him to reconsider his destiny. In fact, Mrs. Whittaker said her husband grew irritated with John Bartak, a crew member who continually read his Bible privately and aloud.

But his protests didn't stop Bartak from reading. Nor did Whittaker's resistance stop the Word from penetrating his soul. Unknown to Whittaker, the soil of his heart was being plowed. For it was one morning after a Bible reading that the sea gull landed on Captain Rickenbacker's head. And at that moment Jim became a believer. . . .

Isn't that just like God? Who would have gone to such extremes to save a soul? Amazing the lengths to which he will go to get our attention. †

FROM: *A GENTLE THUNDER*

JESUS TURNS WATER INTO WINE

On the third day there was a wedding in Cana of Galilee, and the mother of Jesus was there. Now both Jesus and His disciples were invited to the wedding. And when they ran out of wine, the mother of Jesus said to Him, "They have no wine."

Jesus said to her, "Woman, what does your concern have to do with Me? My hour has not yet come."

His mother said to the servants, "Whatever He says to you, do it."

Now there were set there six waterpots of stone, according to the manner of purification of the Jews, containing twenty or thirty gallons apiece.

Jesus said to them, "Fill the waterpots with water." And they filled them up to the brim. And He said to them, "Draw some out now, and take it to the master of the feast." And they took it. When the master of the feast had tasted the water that was made wine, and did not know where it came from (but the servants who had drawn the water knew), the master of the feast called the bridegroom. And he said to him, "Every man at the beginning sets out the good wine, and when the guests have well drunk, then the inferior. You have kept the good wine until now!"

This beginning of signs Jesus did in Cana of Galilee, and manifested His glory; and His disciples believed in Him.

JOHN 2:1–11

‒‒‒‒‒‒⟨⟨⟨∞⟩⟩⟩‒‒‒‒‒‒

Hospitality at a wedding was a sacred duty. So serious were those social customs that, if they were not observed, lawsuits could be brought by the injured parties!

"Without wine," said the rabbis, "there is no joy." Wine was crucial, not for drunkenness, which was considered a disgrace, but for what it demonstrated. The presence of wine stated that this was a special day and that all the guests were special guests. . . .

Mary, the mother of Jesus, is one of the first to notice that the wine has run out. She goes to her Son and points out the problem: "They have no wine."

Jesus' response? "Woman, what does your concern have to do with Me? My hour has not yet come."

Interesting statement. "My hour." Jesus is aware of the plan. He has a place and a time for his first miracle. And this isn't it.

Jesus knows the plan. At first, it appears he is going to stay with it. But as he hears his mother and looks into the faces of the wedding party, he reconsiders. The significance of the plan is slowly eclipsed by his concern for the people. Timing is important, but people are more so.

As a result, he changes his plan to meet the needs of some friends. Incredible. The schedule of heaven is altered so some friends won't be embarrassed. The inaugural miracle is motivated—not by tragedy or famine or moral collapse—but by concern for friends who are in a bind. . . .

His friends were embarrassed. What bothered them bothered him.

So go ahead. Tell God what hurts. Talk to him. He won't turn you away. He won't think it's silly. . . . Does God care about the little things in our lives? You better believe it.

If it matters to you, it matters to him. †

FROM: *HE STILL MOVES STONES*

Jesus Begins His Ministry

Now when Jesus heard that John had been put in prison, He departed to Galilee. And leaving Nazareth, He came and dwelt in Capernaum, which is by the sea, in the regions of Zebulun and Naphtali, that it might be fulfilled which was spoken by Isaiah the prophet, saying:

> *"The land of Zebulun and the land of*
> *Naphtali,*
> *By the way of the sea, beyond the Jordan,*
> *Galilee of the Gentiles:*
> *The people who sat in darkness have seen*
> *a great light,*
> *And upon those who sat in the region*
> *and shadow of death*
> *Light has dawned."*

MATTHEW 4:12–16

He looked around the carpentry shop. He stood for a moment in the refuge of the little room that housed so many sweet memories. He balanced the hammer in his hand. He ran his fingers across the sharp teeth of the saw. He stroked the smoothly worn wood of the sawhorse. He had come to say good-bye.

It was time for him to leave. He had heard something that made him know it was time to go. So he came one last time to smell the sawdust and lumber. Life was peaceful here. Life was so . . . safe.

I wonder what he thought as he took one last look around the room. Perhaps he stood for a moment. Perhaps he listened as voices from the past filled the air. "Good job, Jesus." "Joseph, Jesus—come and eat!" "Don't worry, sir, we'll get it finished on time. I'll get Jesus to help me." I wonder if he hesitated.

You can almost see the tools of the trade in his words as he spoke. You can see the trueness of a plumb line as he called for moral standards. You can imagine him with a pencil and a ledger as he urges honesty. It was here that his human hands shaped the wood his divine hands had created. And it was here that his body matured while his Spirit waited for the right moment, the right day.

And now that day had arrived. ✝

FROM: *GOD CAME NEAR*

Jesus Calls Peter, James, and John

When He had stopped speaking, He said to Simon, "Launch out into the deep and let down your nets for a catch."

But Simon answered and said to Him, "Master, we have toiled all night and caught nothing; nevertheless at Your word I will let down the net." And when they had done this, they caught a great number of fish, and their net was breaking. So they signaled to their partners in the other boat to come and help them. And they came and filled both the boats, so that they began to sink. When Simon Peter saw it, he fell down at Jesus' knees, saying, "Depart from me, for I am a sinful man, O Lord!"

For he and all who were with him were astonished at the catch of fish which they had taken; and so also were James and John, the sons of Zebedee, who were partners with Simon. And Jesus said to Simon, "Do not be afraid. From now on you will catch men." So when they had brought their boats to land, they forsook all and followed Him.

Luke 5:4–11

"Push out into the deep, Peter. Let's fish." I groaned. I looked at John. We were thinking the same thing. As long as he wanted to use the boat for a platform to speak, that was fine. But to use it for a fishing boat—that was our territory. I started to tell this carpenter-teacher, "You stick to preaching, and I'll stick to fishing." But I was more polite: "We worked all night. We didn't catch a thing." . . .

With every pull of the paddle, I grumbled. "No way. No way. Impossible. I may not know much, but I know fishing. And all we're going to come back with are some wet nets."

Finally we cast anchor. I picked up the heavy netting, held it waist-high, and started to throw it. That's when I caught a glimpse of Jesus out of the corner of my eye. His expression stopped me in mid-motion.

He noticed me looking at him, and he tried to hide the smile, but it persisted. . . .

"Boy, is he in for a disappointment," I thought as I threw the net. I wrapped the rope once around my hand and sat back for the long wait.

But there was no wait. The slack rope yanked taut and tried to pull me overboard.

I set my feet against the side of the boat and yelled for help.

We got the net in just before it began to tear. I'd never seen such a catch. We began to take in water. John screamed for the other boat to help us.

It was quite a scene: four fishermen in two boats, knee-deep in fish, and one carpenter seated on our bow, relishing the pandemonium. . . .

It was a scene I would see many times over the next couple of years—in cemeteries with the dead, on hillsides with the hungry, in storms with the frightened, on roadsides with the sick. The characters would change, but the theme wouldn't. When we would say, "No way," he would say, "My way." Then the ones who doubted would scramble to salvage the blessing. And the One who gave it would savor the surprise. †

FROM: *THE APPLAUSE OF HEAVEN*

DAY 6

JESUS' SERMON ON THE MOUNT

And seeing the multitudes, He went up on a mountain, and when He was seated His disciples came to Him. Then He opened His mouth and taught them, saying:

"Blessed are the poor in spirit,
For theirs is the kingdom of heaven.
Blessed are those who mourn,
For they shall be comforted.
Blessed are the meek,
For they shall inherit the earth.
Blessed are those who hunger and thirst
for righteousness,
For they shall be filled.
Blessed are the merciful,
For they shall obtain mercy.
Blessed are the pure in heart,
For they shall see God.
Blessed are the peacemakers,
For they shall be called sons of God.
Blessed are those who are persecuted for
righteousness' sake,
For theirs is the kingdom of heaven."

MATTHEW 5:1–10

Sacred delight is good news coming through the back door of your heart. It's what you'd always dreamed but never expected. It's having God as your pinch-hitter, your lawyer, your dad, your biggest fan, and your best friend. It's hope where you least expected it: a flower in life's sidewalk.

And it is this sacred delight that Jesus promises in the Sermon on the Mount.

Nine times he promises it. And he promises it to an unlikely crowd:

• *"The poor in spirit."* Beggars in God's soup kitchen.

• *"Those who mourn."* Sinners Anonymous bound together by the truth of their introduction: "Hi, I am me. I'm a sinner."

• *"The meek."* Pawnshop pianos played by Van Cliburn. (He's so good no one notices the missing keys.)

• *"Those who hunger and thirst."* Famished orphans who know the difference between a TV dinner and a Thanksgiving feast.

• *"The merciful."* Winners of the million-dollar lottery who share the prize with their enemies.

- *"The pure in heart."* Physicians who love lepers and escape infection.
- *"The peacemakers."* Architects who build bridges with wood from a Roman cross.
- *"Those who are persecuted."* Those who manage to keep an eye on heaven while walking through hell on earth.

It is to this band of pilgrims that God promises a special blessing. A heavenly joy. A sacred delight. †

FROM: *THE APPLAUSE OF HEAVEN*

JESUS TALKS WITH A
SAMARITAN WOMAN

So He came to a city of Samaria which is called Sychar. . . . Now Jacob's well was there. Jesus therefore, being wearied from His journey, sat thus by the well. . . .

A woman of Samaria came to draw water. Jesus said to her, "Give Me a drink." For His disciples had gone away into the city to buy food.

Then the woman of Samaria said to Him, "How is it that You, being a Jew, ask a drink from me, a Samaritan woman?" For Jews have no dealings with Samaritans.

Jesus answered and said to her, "If you knew the gift of God, and who it is who says to you, 'Give Me a drink,' you would have asked Him, and He would have given you living water."

The woman said to Him, "Sir, You have nothing to draw with, and the well is deep. Where then do You get that living water? Are You greater than our father Jacob, who gave us the well, and drank from it himself, as well as his sons and his livestock?"

Jesus answered and said to her, "Whoever drinks of this water will thirst again, but whoever drinks of the water that I shall give him will never thirst. But the water that I shall give him will become in him a fountain of water springing up into everlasting life."

John 4:5–14

～～～

He was seated on the ground: legs outstretched, hands folded, back resting against the well. She stopped and looked at him. He was obviously Jewish. What was he doing here?

Sensing her discomfort, Jesus asked her for water. But she was too streetwise to think that all he wanted was a drink. She wanted to know what he really had in mind. Her intuition was partly correct. He was interested in her heart.

They talked. Who could remember the last time a man had spoken to her with respect? He told her about a spring of water that would quench, not the thirst of the throat, but of the soul.

"Sir, give me this water so that I won't get thirsty and have to keep coming here to draw water."

"Go, call your husband and come back."

Her heart must have sunk. Here was a Jew

who didn't care if she was a Samaritan. Here was the closest thing to gentleness she'd ever seen. And now he was asking her about . . . that. . . .

"I have no husband." (Kindness has a way of inviting honesty.) This woman wondered what Jesus would do. He will be angry. He will leave. He will think I'm worthless. If you've had the same anxieties, then get out your pencil. You'll want to underline Jesus' answer. "You're right. You have had five husbands and the man you are with now won't even give you a name." . . .

Then she asked the question that revealed the gaping hole in her soul. "Where is God? My people say he is on the mountain. Your people say he is in Jerusalem. I don't know where he is." Of all the women to have an insatiable appetite for God—a five-time divorcée? And of all the people to be chosen to personally receive the secret of the ages— an outcast among outcasts? His eyes must have danced as he whispered the secret. "I am the Messiah." †

FROM: *SIX HOURS ONE FRIDAY*

JESUS HEALS A
PARALYZED MAN

And again He entered Capernaum after some days, and it was heard that He was in the house. Immediately many gathered together, so that there was no longer room to receive them, not even near the door. And He preached the word to them. Then they came to Him, bringing a paralytic who was carried by four men. And when they could not come near Him because of the crowd, they uncovered the roof where He was. So when they had broken through, they let down the bed on which the paralytic was lying.

When Jesus saw their faith, He said to the paralytic, "Son, your sins are forgiven you." . . .

Immediately he arose, took up the bed, and went out in the presence of them all, so that all were amazed and glorified God, saying, "We never saw anything like this!"

MARK 2:1–5, 12

It was risky—they could fall. It was dangerous—*he* could fall. It was unorthodox—de-roofing is antisocial. But it was their only chance to see Jesus. So they climbed to the roof.

Faith does those things. Faith does the unexpected. And faith gets God's attention. Look what Mark says: "When Jesus saw their faith, He said to the paralytic, 'Son, your sins are forgiven.'"

The friends want him to heal their friend. But Jesus won't settle for a simple healing of the body—he wants to heal the soul. He leapfrogs the physical and deals with the spiritual. To heal the body is temporal; to heal the soul is eternal.

The request of the friends is valid—but timid. The expectations of the crowd are high—but not high enough. They expect Jesus to say, "I heal you." Instead he says, "I forgive you." . . .

Remarkable. Sometimes God is so touched by what he sees that he gives us what we need and not simply that for which we ask. ✝

FROM: *HE STILL MOVES STONES*

JESUS HEALS JAIRUS'S DAUGHTER

And behold, one of the rulers of the synagogue came, Jairus by name. And when he saw Him, he fell at His feet and begged Him earnestly, saying, "My little daughter lies at the point of death. Come and lay Your hands on her, that she may be healed, and she will live." So Jesus went with him, and a great multitude followed Him and thronged Him. . . .

Then He came to the house of the ruler of the synagogue, and saw a tumult and those who wept and wailed loudly. When He came in, He said to them, "Why make this commotion and weep? The child is not dead, but sleeping."

And they ridiculed Him. But when He had put them all outside, He took the father and the mother of the child, and those who were with Him, and entered where the child was lying. Then He took the child by the hand, and said to her, "Talitha, cumi," which is translated, "Little girl, I say to you, arise." Immediately the girl arose and walked, for she was twelve years of age. And they were overcome with great amazement.

MARK 5:22–24, 38–42

Jairus is the leader of the synagogue. That may not mean much to you and me, but in the days of Christ the leader of the synagogue was the most important man in the community. The synagogue was the center of religion, education, leadership, and social activity. The leader of the synagogue was the senior religious leader, the highest-ranking professor, the mayor, and the best-known citizen all in one.

Who could ask for more? Yet Jairus does. He has to ask for more. In fact, he would trade the whole package of perks and privileges for just one assurance—that his daughter will live.

He fell at Jesus' feet, saying, "My little daughter lies at the point of death. Come and lay Your hands on her that she may be healed, and she will live."

He doesn't barter with Jesus. He doesn't make excuses. He just pleads.

There are times in life when everything you have to offer is nothing compared to what you are asking to receive. What could a man offer in exchange for his child's life? So there are no games. No haggling. No masquerades.

So Jairus asks for his help. And Jesus, who loves the honest heart, goes to give it. †

FROM: *HE STILL MOVES STONES*

DAY 10

JESUS HEALS A SICK WOMAN

Now a certain woman had a flow of blood for twelve years, and had suffered many things from many physicians. She had spent all that she had and was no better, but rather grew worse. When she heard about Jesus, she came behind Him in the crowd and touched His garment. For she said, "If only I may touch His clothes, I shall be made well."

Immediately the fountain of her blood was dried up, and she felt in her body that she was healed of the affliction. And Jesus, immediately knowing in Himself that power had gone out of Him, turned around in the crowd and said, "Who touched My clothes?"

But His disciples said to Him, "You see the multitude thronging You, and You say, 'Who touched Me?'"

And He looked around to see her who had done this thing. But the woman, fearing and trembling, knowing what had happened to her, came and fell down before Him and told Him the whole truth. And He said to her, "Daughter, your faith has made you well. Go in peace, and be healed of your affliction."

MARK 5:25–34

She was a bruised reed: "a flow of blood for twelve years," "suffered many things," "spent all that she had," and "was no better." But for a Jewess, nothing could be worse. No part of her life was left unaffected.

Sexually . . . she could not touch her husband.

Maternally . . . she could not bear children.

Domestically . . . anything she touched was considered unclean. No washing dishes, sweeping floors.

Spiritually . . . she was not allowed to enter the temple.

She was physically exhausted and socially ostracized.

By the time she gets to Jesus, he is surrounded by people. "If only I may touch His clothes," she thinks, "I shall be made well." Risky decision. . . .

Maybe that's all you have: a crazy hunch and a high hope. You have nothing to give. Maybe that has kept you from coming to God. If that describes you, note carefully, only one person was commended that day for having faith. She was a shame-struck, penniless outcast who clutched on to her hunch that he could and her hope that he would. †

FROM: *HE STILL MOVES STONES*

DAY 11

⟨⟨⟨⟩⟩⟩

JESUS' TRANSFIGURATION

Now it came to pass, about eight days after these sayings, that He took Peter, John, and James and went up on the mountain to pray. As He prayed, the appearance of His face was altered, and His robe became white and glistening. And behold, two men talked with Him, who were Moses and Elijah, who appeared in glory and spoke of His decease which He was about to accomplish at Jerusalem. But Peter and those with him were heavy with sleep; and when they were fully awake, they saw His glory and the two men who stood with Him. Then it happened, as they were parting from Him, that Peter said to Jesus, "Master, it is good for us to be here; and let us make three tabernacles: one for You, one for Moses, and one for Elijah"—not knowing what he said.

While he was saying this, a cloud came and overshadowed them; and they were fearful as they entered the cloud. And a voice came out of the cloud, saying, "This is My beloved Son. Hear Him!" When the voice had ceased, Jesus was found alone. But they kept quiet, and told no one in those days any of the things they had seen.

LUKE 9:28–36

⟨⟨⟨⟩⟩⟩

As He prayed," Luke writes, "the appearance of His face was altered, and His robe became white and glistening." For just a moment, he is trans-figured; a roaring radiance pours from him. He becomes as he was before he came. He is elevated above earth's horizon and escorted into the eternal. He is home again. Familiar sounds surround him.

Moses and Elijah, aflame with eternal robes, stand beside their King. When Jesus was preparing himself in the desert for the work of life, angels came to encourage him. Now, on the mountain, preparing himself for the work of death, Moses and Elijah draw near: Moses, the lawgiver whose grave no man knew; Elijah, the prophet who sidestepped death in a fiery chariot.

And then, the voice thunders. God inhabits a cloud. And from the belly of the cloud, the Father speaks: "This is My beloved Son. Hear Him!"

For Peter, James, and John, the scene is bizarre: dazzling white clouds, a voice from the sky, living images from the past. But for Jesus, it is a view of home. . . . A glimpse into tomorrow. †

FROM: *IN THE EYE OF THE STORM*

∞∞

JESUS HEALS A MAN AT THE POOL OF BETHESDA

After this there was a feast of the Jews, and Jesus went up to Jerusalem. Now there is in Jerusalem by the Sheep Gate a pool, which is called in Hebrew, Bethesda, having five porches. In these lay a great multitude of sick people, blind, lame, paralyzed, waiting for the moving of the water. For an angel went down at a certain time into the pool and stirred up the water; then whoever stepped in first, after the stirring of the water, was made well of whatever disease he had. Now a certain man was there who had an infirmity thirty-eight years. When Jesus saw him lying there, and knew that he already had been in that condition a long time, He said to him, "Do you want to be made well?"

The sick man answered Him, "Sir, I have no man to put me into the pool when the water is stirred up; but while I am coming, another steps down before me."

Jesus said to him, "Rise, take up your bed and walk."

JOHN 5:1–8

∞∞

Picture a battleground strewn with wounded bodies, and you see Bethesda. Imagine a nursing home overcrowded and understaffed, and you see the pool. Call to mind the orphans in Bangladesh or the abandoned in New Delhi, and you will see what people saw when they passed Bethesda. As they passed, what did they hear? An endless wave of groans. What did they witness? A faceless field of need. What did they do? Most walked past, ignoring the people.

But not Jesus. He is in Jerusalem for a feast. We don't know if he ever made it to the temple, but we do know he made it to Bethesda. . . .

Can you picture it? Jesus walking among the suffering. What is he thinking? When an infected hand touches his ankle, what does he do? When a blind child stumbles in Jesus' path, does he reach down to catch the child? When a wrinkled hand extends for alms, how does Jesus respond? . . .

How does God feel when people hurt?

It's worth the telling of the story if all we do is watch him walk. It's worth it just to know he even came. †

FROM: *HE STILL MOVES STONES*

JESUS FEEDS THE FIVE THOUSAND

Then Jesus lifted up His eyes, and seeing a great multitude coming toward Him, He said to Philip, "Where shall we buy bread, that these may eat?" But this He said to test him, for He Himself knew what He would do.

Philip answered Him, "Two hundred denarii worth of bread is not sufficient for them, that every one of them may have a little."

One of His disciples, Andrew, Simon Peter's brother, said to Him, "There is a lad here who has five barley loaves and two small fish, but what are they among so many?"

Then Jesus said, "Make the people sit down." Now there was much grass in the place. So the men sat down, in number about five thousand. And Jesus took the loaves, and when He had given thanks He distributed them to the disciples, and the disciples to those sitting down; and likewise of the fish, as much as they wanted.

JOHN 6:5–11

His lunch wasn't much. In fact, it wasn't anything compared to what was needed for more than five thousand people.

He probably wrestled with the silliness of it all. What was one lunch for so many? He probably asked himself if it was even worth the effort.

How far could one lunch go?

I think that's why he didn't give the lunch to the crowd. Instead he gave it to Jesus. Something told him that if he would plant the seed, God would grant the crop.

So he did.

The boy summoned his courage, got up off the grass, and walked into the circle of grownups. He must have been nervous. No one likes to appear silly.

Someone probably snickered.

If they didn't snicker, they shook their heads. "The little fellow doesn't know any better."

If they didn't shake their heads, they rolled their eyes.

But it wasn't the men's heads or eyes that the boy saw; he saw only Jesus. †

FROM: *IN THE EYE OF THE STORM*

DAY 14

JESUS WALKS ON WATER

Now when evening came, His disciples went down to the sea, got into the boat, and went over the sea toward Capernaum. And it was already dark, and Jesus had not come to them. Then the sea arose because a great wind was blowing. So when they had rowed about three or four miles, they saw Jesus walking on the sea and drawing near the boat; and they were afraid. But He said to them, "It is I; do not be afraid." Then they willingly received Him into the boat, and immediately the boat was at the land where they were going.

JOHN 6:16–21

Suppose one of Jesus' disciples kept a journal. And suppose that disciple made an entry in the journal on the morning after the storm. Here is how it would read . . . I suppose:

In the midst of the sea, our boat bounced. The waves slapped it as easily as children would a ball. We were a twig in a whirlpool . . . a leaf in the wind. We were helpless.

"A ghost," someone screamed. A flash of lightning illuminated the sky. For a second I could see its face . . . his face. It was the Master!

He spoke: "Take courage! It is I. Don't be afraid." And, somehow, courage came.

"Lord, if it's you, . . . tell me to come to you on the water." The voice was Peter's. He wasn't being cocky. He was scared. He knew that the boat would soon go down. He knew that Jesus was standing up. And he knew where he wanted to be . . . where we all wanted to be.

"Come on," Jesus invited. So Peter climbed over the side and stepped onto the sea. Jesus radiated light at the end of the trail. Peter stepped toward the light like it was his only hope. He was halfway there when we all heard the thunder. I saw his head turn. He looked up at the sky. And down he went. Boy did he yell!

A hand came through the water sheets and grabbed Peter. Lightning flashed again, and I could see the face of Jesus. Hurt covered his face. It was like he couldn't believe that we couldn't believe. . . .

And I did the only thing I could have done. I fell at his feet and worshiped. I had never seen Jesus as I saw him then. But what I witnessed last night, I know I'll never forget. †

FROM: *IN THE EYE OF THE STORM*

JESUS FORGIVES THE WOMAN
TAKEN IN ADULTERY

Then the scribes and Pharisees brought to Him a woman caught in adultery. And when they had set her in the midst, they said to Him, "Teacher, this woman was caught in adultery, in the very act. Now Moses, in the law, commanded us that such should be stoned. But what do You say?" This they said, testing Him, that they might have something of which to accuse Him. But Jesus stooped down and wrote on the ground with His finger, as though He did not hear.

So when they continued asking Him, He raised Himself up and said to them, "He who is without sin among you, let him throw a stone at her first." And again He stooped down and wrote on the ground. Then those who heard it, being convicted by their conscience, went out one by one, beginning with the oldest even to the last. And Jesus was left alone, and the woman standing in the midst. When Jesus had raised Himself up and saw no one but the woman, He said to her, "Woman, where are those accusers of yours? Has no one condemned you?"

She said, "No one, Lord." And Jesus said to her, "Neither do I condemn you; go and sin no more."

JOHN 8:3–11

oses, in the law, commanded us that such should be stoned. But what do You say?" (v. 5). Pretty cocky, this committee of high ethics. Pretty proud of themselves, these agents of righteousness. This will be a moment they long remember, the morning they foil and snag the mighty Nazarene.

What does Jesus do? Jesus writes in the sand. He stoops down and draws in the dirt. And as he writes, he speaks: "He who is without sin among you, let him throw a stone at her first."

The young look to the old. The old look in their hearts. They are the first to drop their stones. And as they turn to leave, the young who were cocky with borrowed convictions do the same. The only sound is the thud of rocks and the shuffle of feet.

With the jury gone, the courtroom becomes the judge's chambers, and the woman awaits his verdict. "Woman, where are those accusers of yours? Has no one condemned you?" She answers, "No one, Lord." Then Jesus says, "Neither do I condemn you; go and sin no more."

If you have ever wondered how God reacts when you fail, frame these words and hang them on the wall. Read them. Ponder them.

Drink from them. Stand below them and let them wash over your soul.

And remember. Remember the message he left. Not in the sand, but on a cross. Not with his hand, but with his blood. His message has two words: Not guilty. ✝

FROM: *HE STILL MOVES STONES*

JESUS TEACHES FORGIVENESS

Then He said: "A certain man had two sons. And the younger of them said to his father, 'Father, give me the portion of goods that falls to me.' So he divided to them his livelihood. And not many days after, the younger son gathered all together, journeyed to a far country, and there wasted his possessions with prodigal living. But when he had spent all, there arose a severe famine in that land, and he began to be in want. Then he went and joined himself to a citizen of that country, and he sent him into his fields to feed swine. And he would gladly have filled his stomach with the pods that the swine ate, and no one gave him anything.

"But when he came to himself, he said, 'How many of my father's hired servants have bread enough and to spare, and I perish with hunger! I will arise and go to my father, and will say to him, "Father, I have sinned against heaven and before you, and I am no longer worthy to be called your son. Make me like one of your hired servants."'

"And he arose and came to his father. But when he was still a great way off, his father saw him and had compassion, and ran and fell on his neck and kissed him. And the son said to him, 'Father, I have sinned against heaven and in your sight, and am no longer worthy to be called your son.'

"But the father said to his servants, 'Bring out the best robe and put it on him, and put a ring on his hand and sandals on his feet. And bring the fatted calf here and kill it, and let us eat and be merry; for this my son was dead and is alive again; he was lost and is found.' And they began to be merry."

LUKE 15:11–24

———∞∞∞———

He was going home. Not demanding that he get what he deserved, but willing to take whatever he could get. "Give me" had been replaced with "help me," and his defiance had been replaced with repentance.

He had no money. He had no excuses. And he had no idea how much his father had missed him. He had no idea the number of times his father had paused between chores to look out the front gate for his son. The boy had no idea the number of times his father had awakened from restless sleep, gone into the son's room, and sat on the boy's bed.

As the boy came around the bend that led up to the house, he rehearsed his speech one more time. "Father, I have sinned against heaven and against you." . . .

Then he heard the footsteps. Someone was running. *It's probably a servant coming to chase me away or my big brother wanting to know what I'm doing back home.* He began to leave.

But the voice he heard was not the voice of a servant nor the voice of his brother; it was the voice of his father. "Son!" "Father?" Tears glistened on his cheeks as arms stretched from east to west inviting the son to come home.

"Father, I have sinned." The words were muffled as the boy buried his face in his father's shoulder. The two wept. Words were unnecessary. Repentance had been made, forgiveness had been given. The boy was home. †

FROM: *SIX HOURS ONE FRIDAY*

DAY 17

JESUS HEALS THE TEN LEPERS

Now it happened as He went to Jerusalem that He passed through the midst of Samaria and Galilee. Then as He entered a certain village, there met Him ten men who were lepers, who stood afar off. And they lifted up their voices and said, "Jesus, Master, have mercy on us!"

So when He saw them, He said to them, "Go, show yourselves to the priests." And so it was that as they went, they were cleansed.

And one of them, when he saw that he was healed, returned, and with a loud voice glorified God, and fell down on his face at His feet, giving Him thanks. And he was a Samaritan.

So Jesus answered and said, "Were there not ten cleansed? But where are the nine? Were there not any found who returned to give glory to God except this foreigner?" And He said to him, "Arise, go your way. Your faith has made you well."

LUKE 17:11–19

Those who know Christ most are the most grateful. I recently read a story of a woman who for years was married to a harsh husband. Each day he would leave her a list of chores to complete before he returned at the end of the day. "Clean the yard. Stack the firewood. Wash the windows. . . ."

If she didn't complete the tasks, she would be greeted with his explosive anger. But even if she did complete the list, he was never satisfied; he would always find inadequacies in her work.

After several years, the husband passed away. Some time later she remarried, this time to a man who lavished her with tenderness and adoration.

One day, while going through a box of old papers, the wife discovered one of her first husband's lists. And as she read the sheet, a realization caused a tear of joy to splash the paper.

"I'm still doing all these things, and no one has to tell me. I do it because I love him."

That is the unique characteristic of the new kingdom. Its subjects don't work in order to go to heaven: they work because they are going to heaven. Arrogance and fear are replaced with gratitude and joy. †

FROM: *THE APPLAUSE OF HEAVEN*

JESUS RAISES LAZARUS
FROM THE DEAD

Jesus said, "Take away the stone."

Martha, the sister of him who was dead, said to Him, "Lord, by this time there is a stench, for he has been dead four days."

Jesus said to her, "Did I not say to you that if you would believe you would see the glory of God?" Then they took away the stone from the place where the dead man was lying. And Jesus lifted up His eyes and said, "Father, I thank You that You have heard Me. And I know that You always hear Me, but because of the people who are standing by I said this, that they may believe that You sent Me." Now when He had said these things, He cried with a loud voice, "Lazarus, come forth!" And he who had died came out bound hand and foot with graveclothes, and his face was wrapped with a cloth. Jesus said to them, "Loose him, and let him go." . . .

Now a great many of the Jews knew that He was there; and they came, not for Jesus' sake only, but that they might also see Lazarus, whom He had raised from the dead. But the chief priests plotted to put Lazarus to death also, because on account of him many of the Jews went away and believed in Jesus.

JOHN 11:39–44; 12:9–11

Wow! Because of Lazarus many Jews "believed in Jesus." Lazarus has been given a trumpet. He has a testimony to give—and what a testimony he has!

"I was always a good fellow," he would say. "I paid my bills. I loved my sisters. I even enjoyed being around Jesus. But I wasn't one of the followers. I didn't get as close as Peter and James and those guys. I kept my distance. Nothing personal. I just didn't want to get carried away.

"But then I got sick. And then I died. I mean, I died dead. Nothing left. Stone-cold. No life. No breath. Nothing. I died to everything. I saw life from the tomb. And then Jesus called me from the grave. When he spoke, my heart beat and my soul stirred, and I was alive again. And I want you to know he can do the same for you."

If God has called you to be a Lazarus, then testify. Remind the rest of us that we, too, have a story to tell. We, too, have neighbors who are lost. We, too, have died and been resurrected. †

FROM: *A GENTLE THUNDER*

DAY 19

THE TRIUMPHAL ENTRY

Now when they drew near Jerusalem, and came to Bethphage, at the Mount of Olives, then Jesus sent two disciples, saying to them, "Go into the village opposite you, and immediately you will find a donkey tied, and a colt with her. Loose them and bring them to Me. And if anyone says anything to you, you shall say, 'The Lord has need of them,' and immediately he will send them."

MATTHEW 21:1–3

When we all get home, I know what I want to do. There's someone I want to get to know. You go ahead and swap stories with Mary or talk doctrine with Paul. I'll catch up with you soon. But first, I want to meet the guy with the donkey.

I don't know his name or what he looks like. I only know one thing: what he gave. He gave a donkey to Jesus on the Sunday he entered Jerusalem. . . .

When we all get to heaven I want to visit this fellow. I have several questions for him.

How did you know? How did you know it was Jesus who needed a donkey? Did you have a vision? Did you get a telegram? Did an angel appear in your bowl of lentils? . . .

How did it feel? How did it feel to look out and see Jesus on the back of the donkey that lived in your barn? Were you proud? Were you surprised? Were you annoyed?

Did you know? Did you have any idea that your generosity would be used for such a noble purpose? Did it ever occur to you that God was going to ride your donkey? Were you aware that all four Gospel writers would tell your story? Did it ever cross your mind that a couple of millenniums later, a curious preacher in South Texas would be pondering your plight late at night?

And as I ponder yours, I ponder mine. Sometimes I get the impression that God wants me to give him something and sometimes I don't give it because I don't know for sure, and then I feel bad because I've missed my chance. And other times, too few times, I hear him and I obey him and feel honored that a gift of mine would be used to carry Jesus into another place. And still other times I wonder if my little deeds today will make a difference in the long haul.

Maybe you have those questions, too. All of us have a donkey. You and I each have something in our lives, which, if given back to God, could, like the donkey, move Jesus and his story further down the road. Maybe you can sing or hug or program a computer or speak Swahili or write a check.

Whichever, that's your donkey. . . .

That guy who gave Jesus the donkey is just one in a long line of folks who gave little things to a big God. Scripture has quite a gallery of donkey-givers. In fact, heaven may have a shrine to honor God's uncommon use of the common. †

FROM: *AND THE ANGELS WERE SILENT*

JESUS CLEARS THE TEMPLE

Then Jesus went into the temple of God and drove out all those who bought and sold in the temple, and overturned the tables of the money changers and the seats of those who sold doves. And He said to them, "It is written, 'My house shall be called a house of prayer,' but you have made it a 'den of thieves.'"

MATTHEW 21:12–13

I t's a sad but true fact of the faith: religion is used for profit and prestige. When it is there are two results: people are exploited and God is infuriated.

There's no better example of this than what happened at the temple. After he had entered the city on the back of a donkey, Jesus went "into the temple. So when He had looked around at all things, as the hour was already late, He went out to Bethany with the twelve" (Mark 11:11).

The next morning when he returned, "Jesus went into the temple of God and drove out all those who bought and sold in the temple, and overturned the tables of the money changers and the seats of those who sold doves. And He said to them, "It is written, 'My house shall be called a house of prayer,' but you have made it a 'den of thieves.'"

It's not difficult to see what angered Jesus. Pilgrims journeyed days to see God, to witness the holy, to worship His Majesty. But before they were taken into the presence of God, they were taken to the cleaners.

Want to anger God? Get in the way of people who want to see him. Want to feel his fury? Exploit people in the name of God.

Mark it down. Religious hucksters poke the fire of divine wrath.

God will never hold guiltless those who exploit the privilege of worship. ✝

FROM: *AND THE ANGELS WERE SILENT*

JESUS WASHES THE DISCIPLES' FEET

Jesus, knowing that the Father had given all things into His hands, and that He had come from God and was going to God, rose from supper and laid aside His garments, took a towel and girded Himself. After that, He poured water into a basin and began to wash the disciples' feet, and to wipe them with the towel with which He was girded.

JOHN 13:3–5

I don't understand how God can be so kind to us, but he is. He kneels before us, takes our feet in his hands, and washes them. Please understand that in washing the disciples' feet, Jesus is washing ours. That's us being cleansed, not from our dirt, but from our sins.

And the cleansing is not just a gesture; it is a necessity. Listen to what Jesus said: "If I do not wash you, you have no part with Me"

(John 13:8). Why not? Because we cannot. We cannot remove our own sin.

Don't miss the meaning here. To place our feet in the basin of Jesus is to place the filthiest parts of our lives into his hands. In the ancient East, people's feet were caked with mud and dirt. The servant of the feast saw to it that the feet were cleaned. Jesus is assuming the role of the servant. He will wash the grimiest part of your life.

If you let him. The water of the Servant comes only when we confess that we are dirty. Only when we confess that we are caked with filth, that we have walked forbidden trails and followed the wrong paths. We will never be cleansed until we confess we are dirty. And we will never be able to wash the feet of those who have hurt us until we allow Jesus, the one we have hurt, to wash ours. **†**

FROM: *A GENTLE THUNDER*

THE LAST SUPPER

Now on the first day of the Feast of Unleavened Bread the disciples came to Jesus, saying to Him, "Where do You want us to prepare for You to eat the Passover?"

And He said, "Go into the city to a certain man, and say to him, 'The Teacher says, "My time is at hand; I will keep the Passover at your house with My disciples."'"

So the disciples did as Jesus had directed them; and they prepared the Passover.

When evening had come, He sat down with the twelve. . . .

And as they were eating, Jesus took bread, blessed and broke it, and gave it to the disciples and said, "Take, eat; this is My body."

Then He took the cup, and gave thanks, and gave it to them, saying, "Drink from it, all of you. For this is My blood of the new covenant, which is shed for many for the remission of sins. But I say to you, I will not drink of this fruit of the vine from now on until that day when I drink it new with you in My Father's kingdom."

And when they had sung a hymn, they went out to the Mount of Olives.

MATTHEW 26:17–20, 26–30

When you read Matthew's account of the Last Supper, one incredible truth surfaces. Jesus is the person behind it all. It was Jesus who selected the place, designated the time, and set the meal in order. "The chosen time is near. I will have the Passover with my followers at your house."

And at the Supper, Jesus is not a guest, but the host: "[Jesus] gave it to the disciples." The subject of the verbs is the message of the event: he "took" . . . he "blessed" . . . he "broke" . . . he "gave." . . .

And, at the Supper, Jesus is not the served, but the servant. It is Jesus who, during the Supper, put on the garb of a servant and washed the disciples' feet.

Jesus is the most active one at the table. He does not recline and receive, but stands and gives. He still does. The Lord's Supper is a gift to you. The Lord's Supper is a sacrament, not a sacrifice. . . .

He fulfilled his role as a servant by washing their feet. And he fulfilled his role as a Savior by granting them forgiveness of sins.

He was in charge. He was on center stage. He was the person behind and in the moment. And he still is. ✝

FROM: *AND THE ANGELS WERE SILENT*

JESUS PRAYS IN THE GARDEN OF GETHSEMANE

Then Jesus came with them to a place called Gethsemane, and said to the disciples, "Sit here while I go and pray over there." And He took with Him Peter and the two sons of Zebedee, and He began to be sorrowful and deeply distressed. Then He said to them, "My soul is exceedingly sorrowful, even to death. Stay here and watch with Me."

He went a little farther and fell on His face, and prayed, saying, "O My Father, if it is possible, let this cup pass from Me; nevertheless, not as I will, but as You will."

Then He came to His disciples and said to them, "Are you still sleeping and resting? Behold, the hour is at hand, and the Son of Man is being betrayed into the hands of sinners. Rise, let us be going. See, My betrayer is at hand."

MATTHEW 26:36–39, 45–46

My father taught me the lesson early: Don't create havoc in the garden. You can play ball in the yard. You can have races in the alley. You can build a fort in the tree. But the garden? Leave it alone.

I hate to think I have anything in common with the devil, but I guess I do. Satan learned the same lesson: Don't mess around with a garden—especially a garden that belongs to the Father.

The Bible is the story of two gardens. Eden and Gethsemane. In the first, Adam took a fall. In the second, Jesus took a stand. In the first, God sought Adam. In the second, Jesus sought God. In Eden, Adam hid from God. In Gethsemane, Jesus emerged from the dark. In Eden, Satan led Adam to a tree that led to his death. From Gethsemane, Jesus went to a tree that led to our life.

Satan was never invited to the Garden of Eden. He did not belong there. If he has invaded a garden of your life, then invite Jesus to reclaim it. Open the gate to God. He will enter and do what he did at Gethsemane. He will pray, and he will protect, and he will reclaim. †

FROM: *A GENTLE THUNDER*

JESUS IS ARRESTED

Jesus therefore, knowing all things that would come upon Him, went forward and said to them, "Whom are you seeking?"

They answered Him, "Jesus of Nazareth." Jesus said to them, "I am He." And Judas, who betrayed Him, also stood with them. Now when He said to them, "I am He," they drew back and fell to the ground.

Then He asked them again, "Whom are you seeking?"

And they said, "Jesus of Nazareth."

Jesus answered, "I have told you that I am He. Therefore, if you seek Me, let these go their way."

JOHN 18:4–8

Remarkable. They stand only a few feet from his face and don't recognize him. Not even Judas realizes who stands before them. What a truth. Seeing Jesus is more than a matter of the eyes; it is a matter of the heart. The enemy is next to Jesus and doesn't even realize it.

He reveals himself. "I am He." His voice flicks the first domino, and down they tumble. Were the moment not so solemn it would be comic. These are the best soldiers with Satan's finest plan; yet one word from Jesus, and they fall down! Don't miss the symbolism here: When Jesus speaks, Satan falls. Doesn't matter who the evil one has recruited. The best of Satan melts as wax before the presence of Christ.

Jesus has to ask them again whom they seek. "Whom are you seeking?" When they answer that they are looking for Jesus of Nazareth, he instructs them, "If you seek Me, let these go their way." ✝

FROM: *A GENTLE THUNDER*

PILATE QUESTIONS JESUS

Now Jesus stood before the governor. And the governor asked Him, saying, "Are You the King of the Jews?" Jesus said to him, "It is as you say." And while He was being accused by the chief priests and elders, He answered nothing.

Then Pilate said to Him, "Do You not hear how many things they testify against You?" But He answered him not one word, so that the governor marveled greatly.

Now at the feast the governor was accustomed to releasing to the multitude one prisoner whom they wished. And at that time they had a notorious prisoner called Barabbas. Therefore, when they had gathered together, Pilate said to them, "Whom do you want me to release to you? Barabbas, or Jesus who is called Christ?" For he knew that they had handed Him over because of envy.

While he was sitting on the judgment seat, his wife sent to him, saying, "Have nothing to do with that just Man, for I have suffered many things today in a dream because of Him."

But the chief priests and elders persuaded the multitudes that they should ask for

Barabbas and destroy Jesus. The governor answered and said to them, "Which of the two do you want me to release to you?"

They said, "Barabbas!"

Pilate said to them, "What then shall I do with Jesus who is called Christ?"

They all said to him, "Let Him be crucified!"

Then the governor said, "Why, what evil has He done?"

But they cried out all the more, saying, "Let Him be crucified!"

When Pilate saw that he could not prevail at all, but rather that a tumult was rising, he took water and washed his hands before the multitude, saying, "I am innocent of the blood of this just Person. You see to it."

And all the people answered and said, "His blood be on us and on our children."

Then he released Barabbas to them; and when he had scourged Jesus, he delivered Him to be crucified.

MATTHEW 27:11–26

Perhaps you, like Pilate, are curious about this one called Jesus. Pilate's question is yours. "What will I do with this man, Jesus?"

You have two choices. You can reject him. That is an option. You can, as have many, decide that the idea of God becoming a carpenter is too bizarre—and walk away. Or you can accept him. You can journey with him. You can listen for his voice amidst the hundreds of voices and follow him.

Pilate could have. He heard many voices that day—he could have heard Christ's. Had Pilate chosen to respond to this bruised Messiah, his story would have been different. Listen to his question: "Are You the King of the Jews?" Had we been there that day we would know the tone of voice Pilate used. Mockery? (You . . . the king?) Curiosity? (Who are you?) Sincerity? (Are you really who you say you are?) We wonder about his motive. So did Jesus.

"Is that your own question, or did others tell you about me?" Jesus wants to know why Pilate wants to know. What if Pilate had simply said, "I'm asking for myself. I want to know. I really want to know. Are you the king you claim to be?" If he had asked,

Jesus would have told him. If he had asked, Jesus would have freed him. But Pilate didn't want to know. He just turned on his heel and retorted, "I am not Jewish." Pilate didn't ask so Jesus didn't tell. . . .

Legend has it that Pilate's wife became a believer. And legend has it that Pilate's eternal home is a mountain lake where he daily surfaces, still plunging his hands into the water seeking forgiveness. Forever trying to wash away his guilt . . . not for the evil he did, but for the kindness he didn't do. ✝

FROM: *AND THE ANGELS WERE SILENT*

DAY 26

Jesus' Crucifixion

Now when the sixth hour had come, there was darkness over the whole land until the ninth hour. And at the ninth hour Jesus cried out with a loud voice, saying, "Eloi, Eloi, lama sabachthani?" which is translated, "My God, My God, why have You forsaken Me?"

Some of those who stood by, when they heard that, said, "Look, He is calling for Elijah!" Then someone ran and filled a sponge full of sour wine, put it on a reed, and offered it to Him to drink, saying, "Let Him alone; let us see if Elijah will come to take Him down."

And Jesus cried out with a loud voice, and breathed His last.

Then the veil of the temple was torn in two from top to bottom. So when the centurion, who stood opposite Him, saw that He cried out like this and breathed His last, he said, "Truly this Man was the Son of God!"

MARK 15:33–39

They killed him. He left as he came—penniless. He was buried in a borrowed grave, his funeral financed by compassionate friends. Though he once had everything, he died with nothing.

He should have been miserable. He should have been bitter. He had every right to be a pot of boiling anger. But he wasn't. . . .

People followed him wherever he went. Children scampered after this man. . . . Crowds clamored to hear him.

Why? He was joyful. He was joyful when he was poor. He was joyful when he was abandoned. He was joyful when he was betrayed. He was even joyful as he hung on a tool of torture, his hands pierced with six-inch Roman spikes. Jesus embodied a stubborn joy. A joy that refused to bend in the wind of hard times. A joy that held its ground against pain. A joy whose roots extended deep into the bedrock of eternity. . . .

What is this cheerfulness that dares to wink at adversity? What is this bird that sings while it is still dark? What is the source of this peace that defies pain?

I call it sacred delight. . . . What is sacred is God's. And this joy is God's. †

FROM: *THE APPLAUSE OF HEAVEN*

THE RESURRECTION

And behold, there was a great earthquake; for an angel of the Lord descended from heaven, and came and rolled back the stone from the door, and sat on it. His countenance was like lightning, and his clothing as white as snow. And the guards shook for fear of him, and became like dead men.

But the angel answered and said to the women, "Do not be afraid, for I know that you seek Jesus who was crucified. He is not here; for He is risen, as He said. Come, see the place where the Lord lay. And go quickly and tell His disciples that He is risen from the dead, and indeed He is going before you into Galilee; there you will see Him. Behold, I have told you."

So they went out quickly from the tomb with fear and great joy, and ran to bring His disciples word.

And as they went to tell His disciples, behold, Jesus met them, saying, "Rejoice!" So they came and held Him by the feet and worshiped Him. Then Jesus said to them, "Do not be afraid. Go and tell My brethren to go to Galilee, and there they will see Me."

MATTHEW 28:2–10

Why did the angel move the stone? For whom did he roll away the rock? For Jesus? Did the stone have to be removed for Jesus to exit? Did God have to help? Was the death conqueror so weak that he couldn't push away a rock? . . .

Listen to what the angel says: "Come and see the place where his body was."

The stone was moved! . . .

Mary looks at Mary and Mary is grinning the same grin she had when the bread and fish kept coming out of the basket. Suddenly it's all right to dream again.

"Go quickly and tell His disciples that He is risen from the dead, and indeed He is going before you into Galilee. . . ."

Mary and Mary don't have to be told twice. The sun is up. The Son is out. But the Son isn't finished.

One surprise still awaits them.

"Behold, Jesus met them, saying, 'Rejoice!' So they came and held Him by the feet and worshiped Him. Then Jesus said to them, 'Do not be afraid. Go and tell My brethren to go to Galilee, and there they will see Me.'" †

FROM: *HE STILL MOVES STONES*

The Road to Emmaus

Now behold, two of them were traveling that same day to a village called Emmaus, which was seven miles from Jerusalem. And they talked together of all these things which had happened. So it was, while they conversed and reasoned, that Jesus Himself drew near and went with them. But their eyes were restrained, so that they did not know Him.

And He said to them, "What kind of conversation is this that you have with one another as you walk and are sad?"

Then the one whose name was Cleopas answered and said to Him, "Are You the only stranger in Jerusalem, and have You not known the things which happened there in these days?"

And He said to them, "What things?"

So they said to Him, "The things concerning Jesus of Nazareth, who was a Prophet mighty in deed and word before God and all the people, and how the chief priests and our rulers delivered Him to be condemned to death, and crucified Him. But we were hoping that it was He who was going to redeem Israel. . . ."

Then He said to them, "O foolish ones, and slow of heart to believe in all that the prophets have spoken! Ought not the Christ to have suffered these things and to enter into His glory?" And beginning at Moses and all the Prophets, He expounded to them in all the Scriptures the things concerning Himself.

LUKE 24:13–27

⟶⟳⟵

T wo disciples are walking down the dusty road to the village of Emmaus. Their talk concerns the crucified Jesus. "I can hardly believe it. He's gone." "What do we do now?"

Just then a stranger comes up from behind and says, "I'm sorry, but I couldn't help overhearing you. Who are you discussing?" They stop and turn.

One of them asks, "Where have you been the last few days? Haven't you heard about Jesus of Nazareth?" And he continues to tell what has happened.

This scene fascinates me—two sincere disciples telling how the last nail has been driven in Israel's coffin. God, in disguise, listens patiently, his wounded hands buried deeply in his robe.

He must have been touched at the faithfulness of this pair. Yet he also must have been a bit chagrined. He had just gone to hell and back to give heaven to earth, and these two were worried about the political situation of Israel.

"But we were hoping that it was He who was going to redeem Israel."

Words painted gray with disappointment. What we wanted didn't come. What came, we didn't want. The result? Shattered hope. The foundation of their world trembles.

We are not much different than burdened travelers, are we?

Our problem is not so much that God doesn't give us what we hope for as it is that we don't know the right thing for which to hope. (You may want to read that sentence again.)

Hope is not a granted wish or a favor performed; no, it is far greater than that. It is a zany, unpredictable dependence on a God who loves to surprise us out of our socks and be there in the flesh to see our reaction. ✝

FROM: *GOD CAME NEAR*

JESUS CALLS PAUL

Then Saul, still breathing threats and murder against the disciples of the Lord, went to the high priest and asked letters from him to the synagogues of Damascus, so that if he found any who were of the Way, whether men or women, he might bring them bound to Jerusalem.

As he journeyed he came near Damascus, and suddenly a light shone around him from heaven. Then he fell to the ground, and heard a voice saying to him, "Saul, Saul, why are you persecuting Me?"

And he said, "Who are You, Lord?"

Then the Lord said, "I am Jesus, whom you are persecuting. It is hard for you to kick against the goads."

So he, trembling and astonished, said, "Lord, what do You want me to do?"

Then the Lord said to him, "Arise and go into the city, and you will be told what you must do."

ACTS 9:1–6

Blue-blooded and wild-eyed, this young zealot was hell-bent on keeping the kingdom pure—and that meant keeping the Christians out. He marched through the countryside like a general demanding that backslidden Jews salute the flag of the motherland or kiss their family and hopes good-bye.

All this came to a halt, however, on the shoulder of a highway. Equipped with subpoenas, handcuffs, and a posse, Paul was on his way to do a little personal evangelism in Damascus. That's when someone slammed on the stadium lights, and he heard the voice.

When he found out whose voice it was, his jaw hit the ground, and his body followed. He braced himself for the worst.

Jesus could have finished him on the road. He could have left him for the buzzards. He could have sent him to hell. But he didn't. He sent him to the lost.

Paul himself called it crazy. He described it with phrases like "stumbling block" and "foolishness," but chose in the end to call it "grace."

And he defended his unquenchable loyalty by saying, "The love of Christ compels us" (2 Cor. 5:14).

The message is gripping: Show a man his failures without Jesus, and the result will be found in the roadside gutter. Give a man religion without reminding him of his filth, and the result will be arrogance in a three-piece suit. But get the two in the same heart—get sin to meet Savior and Savior to meet sin—and the result just might be another Pharisee turned preacher who sets the world on fire. †

FROM: *THE APPLAUSE OF HEAVEN*

A VIEW OF HEAVEN

Therefore we do not lose heart. Even though our outward man is perishing, yet the inward man is being renewed day by day. For our light affliction, which is but for a moment, is working for us a far more exceeding and eternal weight of glory, while we do not look at the things which are seen, but at the things which are not seen. For the things which are seen are temporary, but the things which are not seen are eternal.

2 CORINTHIANS 4:16–18

A grand scene awaits you. . . . The Hebrew writer gives us a *National Geographic* piece on heaven. Listen to how he describes the mountaintop of Zion. He says when we reach the mountain we will have to come to "the city of the living God . . . to an innumerable company of angels . . . and church of the firstborn who are registered in heaven, to God the Judge of all, to the spirits of just men made perfect, to Jesus the

Mediator of the new covenant, and to the blood of sprinkling that speaks better things than that of Abel" (Heb. 12:22–24).

What a mountain! Won't it be great to see the angels? To finally know what they look like and who they are? To hear them tell of the times they were at our side, even in our house?

Imagine the meeting of the firstborn. A gathering of all God's children. No jealousy. No competition. No division. No hurry. We will be perfect . . . sinless.

And imagine seeing God. Finally, to gaze in the face of your Father. To feel the Father's gaze upon you.

He will do what he promised he would do. *I will make all things new*, he promised. *I will restore what was taken. I will restore the smiles faded by hurt. I will replay the symphonies unheard by deaf ears and the sunsets unseen by blind eyes. The mute will sing. The poor will feast.*

I will make all things new. New hope. New faith. And most of all new Love. The Love before which all other loves pale. The Love you have sought in a thousand ports in a thousand nights . . . this Love of mine, will be yours. . . .

What a mountain! Jesus will be there. . . .
Believe me when I say it will be worth it.
No cost is too high. Whatever it takes, do it.
For heaven's sake, do it. It will be worth it. I
promise. One view of the peak will justify the
pain of the path. ✝

FROM: *WHEN GOD WHISPERS YOUR NAME*

ACKNOWLEDGMENTS

Grateful acknowledgment is made for the use of copyrighted material from the following books, all by Max Lucado.

And the Angels Were Silent (Nashville: Thomas Nelson, Inc., 2009)

The Applause of Heaven (Nashville: Thomas Nelson, Inc., 2008)

A Gentle Thunder (Nashville: Thomas Nelson, Inc., 2009)

God Came Near (Nashville: Thomas Nelson, Inc., 2010)

He Still Moves Stones (Nashville: Thomas Nelson, Inc., 2009)

In the Eye of the Storm (Nashville: Thomas Nelson, Inc., 2009)

Six Hours One Friday (Nashville: Thomas Nelson, Inc., 2009)

When God Whispers Your Name (Nashville: Thomas Nelson, Inc., 2009)